Preface:

Over the last few years, this book has become one of the most useful books on Numerical Methods using C++. This book has been prepared in accordance with the syllabus of most of the renowned Universities. The detailed concept based approach has made this book an epitome and hallmark in the field of Numerical methods. It is hoped that this will definitely help all sections of the students.

- Authors

Ex. No: 1   Write a C++ program to find the integral value of x^2 using Trapezoidal Method

Date:

AIM:

To find the integral value for the following using Trapezoidal Method.

Integration over x^2 for the limits 0 to 2.

SOURCE CODE:

```cpp
#include<iostream.h>

#include<conio.h>

#include<math.h>

#define f(x) (pow(x,2))

void main()

{
  int i,n;

  float a,b,x[30],y[3];

  double h,l1;

  clrscr();

  cout<<"Enter the lower and upper limit:\n";

  cin>>a>>b;

  cout<<"Enter the number of sub-intervals:\n";

  cin>>n;

  h=(b-a)/n;

  x[0]=a;

  for( i=0; i<n+1; i++)

  {
    y[i]=f(x[i]);
```

```cpp
        if(i==n)
         goto line;
         x[i+1]=x[i]+h;
    }
    line:
    l1=0;
    for( i=0; i<n; i++)
    l1=l1+(h/2)*(y[i]+y[i+1]);
    cout<<"Integral of (x*x) over the interval ( " <<a<<" , "<<b<< " )";
    cout<<endl;
    cout<<"Trapezoidal Rule :\n";
    cout<<l1<<endl;
    getch();
}
```

OUTPUT:

Enter the lower and upper limits:

0   1

Enter the number of sub-intervals:

10

Integral of (x*x) over the interval (0,1)

Trapezoidal Rule:

0.335

Ex. No: 2   **Write a C++ program to find the solution of y'=xz+2 and z'=xy+2 using**
Date: **Runga Kutta Simultaneous Equation**

AIM:

To find the solution of the above given equation using Euler's Method – Runga Kutta Simultaneous Equation Method.

SOURCE CODE:

```
#include<iostream.h>

#include<conio.h>

#include<math.h>

#define f(x, y, z) (x*z+2)

#define g(x, y, z) (x*y+2)

void main()

{

    int i;

    float h, k1, k2, k3, k4, l1, l2, l3, l4, x[10], y[10], z[10];

    clrscr();

    cout<< "Enter the initial values of x, y, z:\n";

    cin>>x[0]>>y[0]>>z[0];

    cout<< "Enter the step size h:\n";

    cin>>h;

    cout<<endl;

    cout<< "Runga Kutta Method – Solution of equation\n";

    cout<< "y'=xz+2 and z'=xy+2"<<endl;

    cout<< "x\t"<< "y\t\t"<< "z\t"<<endl;

    for( i=0; i<10; i++)

    {
```

```cpp
k1=h*f(x[i], y[i], z[i]);

l1=h*g(x[i], y[i], z[i]);

k2=h*f((x[i]+h/2), (y[i]+k1/2), (z[i]+l1/2));

l2=h*g((x[i]+h/2), (y[i]+k1/2), (z[i]+l1/2));

k3=h*f((x[i]+h/2), (y[i]+k2/2), (z[i]+l2/2));

l3=h*g((x[i]+h/2), (y[i]+k2/2), (z[i]+l2/2));

k4=h*f((x[i]+h), (y[i]+k3), (z[i]+l3));

l4=h*g((x[i]+h), (y[i]+k3), (z[i]+l3));

y[i+1]=y[i]+(k1+2*k2+2*k3+k4)/6;

z[i+1]=z[i]+(l1+2*l2+2*l3+l4)/6;

x[i+1]=x[i]+h;

cout<<x[i+1]<< "\t"<<y[i+1]<< "\t"<< z[i+1]<<endl;
}

getch();

}
```

OUTPUT:

Enter the initial value x, y, z:

0   1   1

Enter the step size h:

0.05

Runga Kutta Method – Solution of Equations

y'=xz+2 and z'=xy+2

x	y	z
0.05	1.101334	1.101334
0.1	1.205681	1.205681
0.15	1.313574	1.313574
0.2	1.425578	1.425578
0.25	1.542292	1.542292
0.3	1.664356	1.664356
0.35	1.792461	1.792461
0.4	1.927351	1.927351
0.45	2.069836	2.069836
0.5	2.220801	2.220801

Ex. No: 3   **Write a C program to fit an equation for the following data**

Date:

X	1	2	3	4	5	6	7	8	9
Y	2	6	7	8	10	5	8	10	20

AIM:

To write a C program to fit a given set of data for X and Y

SOURCE CODE:

```c
#include <stdio.h>

#include <conio.h>

void main ( )

{

  int i, n, j;

  float x[10], y[10], s1=0, s2=0, s3=0, s4=0, d, a, b;

  clrscr ( );

  printf ("Enter the value of n\n");

  scanf ("%d", &n);

  printf ("Enter the values of x and y: \n");

  for (i=0; i<n ; i++)

  {

    scanf ("%f %f", &x[i] , &y[i] );

  }

  for (i=0; i<n; i++)

  {

    s1 = s1 + x[i] ;

    s2 = s2 + x[i]*x[i] ;

    s3 = s3 + y[i] ;
```

```c
    s4 = s4 + x[i]*y[i] ;

}

d = n*s2 – s1*s1 ;

a  = (s2*s3 – s1*s4)/d ;

b = (n*s4 – s1*s3)/d ;

printf ("The value of a and b are: %f and %f \n", a, b);

printf ("The required linear relation is: \n \n");

if ( b > 0 )

  printf (" y = %f + %f x", a, b);

else

  printf (" y = %f %f x" , a, b);

  getch ( );

}
```

OUTPUT:

Enter the value of n

9

Enter the value of x and y

1	2	3	4	5	6	7	8	9
2	6	7	8	10	5	8	10	20

The value of a and b are: 1.527778 and 1.383333

The required linear relation is

y = 1.527778 + 1.383333 x

Ex. No: 4   Write a C++ program to find the largest negative root using Newton-Raphson

Date: method for $3x^3+9x^2-8=0$

AIM:

To write a C++ program to find the largest negative root using Newton-Raphson method for $3x^3+9x^2-8=0$

SOURCE CODE:

```
#include<iostream.h>

#include<conio.h>

#include<math.h>

#define f(x) (3*pow(x,3)+9*pow(x,2)-8)

#define g(x) (9*pow(x,2)+18*x)

void main()

{

int i;

float a,b,f[10],g[10],x[10];

clrscr();

a=0;

read:

b=a-1;

if(f(a)*f(b)>0)

{

a=b;

goto read;

}

else
```

```cpp
x[0]=a;
for(i=0;i<10;i++)
{
f[i]=f(x[i]);
g[i]=g(x[i]);
x[i+1]=x[i]-(f[i]/g[i]);
if(fabs(x[i+1]-x[i])<pow(10,-6))
goto write;
}
write:
cout<<"The negative root of 3*x^3+9*x^2-8=0 is: "<<x[i]<<endl;
getch();
}
```

OUTPUT:

The negative root of 3*x^3+9*x^2-8=0 is: -1.226074

Ex. No: 5   Write a C++ program to find the solution of the following equation by

Date: Gauss Elimination method

$$4x-9y+2z=49;$$

$$2x-4y+5z=4;$$

$$x-y+2z=0;$$

AIM:

To write a C++ program to find the solution of the following equation by Gauss Elimination method.

SOURCE CODE:

```cpp
#include<iostream.h>

#include<conio.h>

#include<math.h>

void main()

{

int i,j,k,n;

float x[10],a[10][10],c[10];

clrscr();

cout<<"Enter the value of n:"<<endl;

cin>>n;

cout<<"Enter the right hand side constants:"<<endl;

for(i=0;i<n;i++)

cin>>c[i];

cout<<"Enter the coefficients row wise:"<<endl;

for(i=0;i<n;i++)

{

for(j=0;j<n;j++)
```

```cpp
    cin>>a[i][j];
    }
    for(k=0;k<n-1;k++)
    {
    for(i=k+1;i<n;i++)
    {
    for(j=k+1;j<n;j++)
    a[i][j]=a[i][j]-(a[i][k]/a[k][k])*a[k][j];
    c[i]=c[i]-(a[i][k]/a[k][k])*c[k];
    }
    }
    x[n-1]=c[n-1]/a[n-1][n-1];
    cout<<"The solution is:"<<endl;
    cout<<"x["<<n-1<<"]"<<x[n-1]<<endl;
    for(k=0;k<n-1;k++)
    {
    i=n-k-2;
    for(j=i+1;j<n;j++)
    c[i]=c[i]-(a[i][j]*x[j]);
    x[i]=c[i]/a[i][i];
    cout<<"x["<<i<<"]="<<x[i]<<endl;
    }
    getch();
    }
```

OUTPUT:

Enter the value of n:

3

Enter the right hand side constants:

49   4   -5

Enter the coefficients row wise:

4   -9   2

2   -4   5

1   -1   3

The solution is:

x[2]=-4.588235

x[1]=-4.294117

x[0]=4.882355

Ex. No: 6   Write a C++ program to find the solution of the following equation by

Date: Gauss -Jordon method

$$x+y+2z=4;$$

$$2x-y+3z=9;$$

$$3x+y+z=1;$$

AIM:

To write a C++ program to find the solution of the following equation by Gauss-Jordon method.

SOURCE CODE:

```cpp
#include<iostream.h>

#include<conio.h>

#include<math.h>

void main()

{

int i,j,k,n;

float x[10],a[10][10];

clrscr();

cout<<"Enter the value of n:"<<endl;

cin>>n;

cout<<"Enter the right hand side constants"<<endl;

for(i=0;i<n;i++)

cin>>a[i][n];

cout<<"Enter the coefficients row wise:"<<endl;

for(i=0;i<n;i++)

{

 for(j=0;j<n;j++)
```

```cpp
    cin>>a[i][j];
    }
    for(k=0;k<n;k++)
    {
    for(i=0;i<n;i++)
    {
    if(i!=k)
    {
    for(j=k+1;j<n+1;j++)
    a[i][j]=a[i][j]-(a[i][k]/a[k][k])*a[k][j];
        }
    }
    }
    cout<<"The solution is:"<<endl;
    for(i=0;i<n;i++)
    {
    x[i]=(a[i][n]/a[i][i]);
    cout<<"x["<<i<<"]="<<x[i]<<endl;
    }
    getch();
    }
```

OUTPUT:

Enter the value of n:

3

Enter the right hand side constants:

4   9   1

Enter the coefficients row wise:

1   1   2

2   -1   3

3   1   1

The solution is:

x[0]=-0.153846

x[1]=-1.230769

x[2]=2.692308

Ex. No: 7   Write a C++ program to find the inverse of the following matrix by

Date: Gauss - Jordon method

$$\begin{matrix} 1 & 1 & 1 \\ 5 & 6 & 8 \\ 10 & 9 & 7 \end{matrix}$$

AIM:

To write a C++ program to find the inverse of the following matrix by Gauss-Jordon method.

SOURCE CODE:

```cpp
#include<iostream.h>
#include<conio.h>
#include<math.h>
void main()
{
int i,j,k,n;
float x[10],a[10][10];
clrscr();
cout<<"Enter the value of n:"<<endl;
cin>>n;
cout<<"Enter the matrix row wise:"<<endl;
for(i=0;i<n;i++)
{
for(j=0;j<n;j++)
cin>>a[i][j];
}
for(i=0;i<n;i++)
{
```

```
for(j=0;j<n;j++)

{

  if(i==j)

  a[i][n+j]=1;

  else

  a[i][n+j]=0;

  }

}

for(k=0;k<n;k++)

{

  for(i=0;i<n;i++)

  {

    if(i!=0)

    {

      for(j=k+1;j<2*n;j++)

      a[i][j]=a[i][j]-(a[i][k]/a[k][k])*a[k][j];

    }

  }

}

for(i=0;i<n;i++)

{

  if(a[i][j]==0)

  {

    cout<<"Inverse does not exist"<<endl;

    goto end;

  }
```

```
    }
cout<<"The inverse of the matrix:"<<endl;
for(i=0;i<n;i++)
{
 for(j=n;j<2*n;j++)
 {
  a[i][j]=(a[i][j]/a[i][i]);
  cout<<a[i][j]<<"\t";
 }
 cout<<endl;
 }
end:
getch();
 }
```

OUTPUT:

Enter the value of n:

3

Enter the matrix row wise:

1	1	1
5	6	8
10	9	7

The inverse does not exist

Ex. No: 8   **Write a C++ program to find the solution for above equations**

Date: **using Gauss Seidal Iteration Method**

$$10x+2y+2z=6; \quad -x-y+5z=5; \quad -x-y+10z=8;$$

AIM:

To find the solution for the above equation using Gauss Seidal Iteration Method.

SOURCE CODE:

```cpp
#include<iostream.h>
#include<conio.h>
#include<math.h>
void main()
{
int i,j,m,n,l;
float x[10],a[10][10],b[10],c;
clrscr();
cout<<"Enter the values of n:"<<endl;
cin>>n;
cout<<"Enter the no of iteration:"<<endl;
cin>>l;
cout<<"Enter the right hand side constants:"<<endl;
for(i=0;i<n;i++)
cin>>b[i];
cout<<"Enter the coefficient row wise:"<<endl;
for(i=0;i<n;i++)
{
x[1]=0;
```

```cpp
for(j=0;j<n;j++)

cin>>a[i][j];

}m=1;

line:

for(i=0;i<n;i++)

{

c=b[i];

for(j=0;j<n;j++)

{

if(i!=j)

c=c-a[i][j]*x[j];

}

x[i]=c/a[i][i];

}

m=m+1;

if(m<=1)

goto line;

else

{

cout<<"The solution is:"<<endl;

for(i=0;i<n;i++)

cout<<"x("<<i<<")="<<x[i]<<endl;

}

getch();

}
```

OUTPUT:

Enter the values of n:

3

Enter the number of iterations:

100

Enter the right hand side constants:

6   5   8

Enter the coefficients of row wise:

10   2   2

-1   -1   5

-1   -1   10

The solution is

x(0)=0.6

x(1)=5.6

x(2)=-0.3

Ex. No: 9   Write a C++ program to find the integration over y^3 dy for the
Date: limits 0 to 1 Simpson's Rule

AIM:

To find the integration over y^3 dy for the limits 0 to 1 using Simpson's Rule.

SOURCE CODE:

```
#include<iostream.h>

#include<conio.h>

#include<math.h>

#define f(x) (pow(x,3))

void main()

{

int i,n;

float a,b,x[30],y[30];

double h,l1;

clrscr();

cout<<"Enter the lower and upper limit:"<<endl;

cin>>a>>b;

cout<<"Enter the no of sub intervals (multiple of 6 not exceeding 30)"<<endl;

cin>>n;

h=(b-a)/n;

x[0]=a;

for(i=0;i<n+1;i++)

{

y[i]=f(x[i]);
```

```
if(i==n)
goto line;
x[i+1]=x[i]+h;
}
line:
l1=0;
for(i=0;i<n-1;i+=2)
l1=l1+(h/3)*(y[i]+4*y[i+1]+y[i+2]);
cout<<"integral of (x^3)over the interval<<"("<<a<<","<<b<<")";
cout<<endl;
cout<<"Simphson's Rule:"<<endl;
cout<<l1<<endl;
getch();
}
```

OUTPUT:

Enter the lower and upper limits:

0   1

Enter the no of sub-intervals(multiple of 6 not exceeding 30)

12

Integral of (x^3) over the interval (0,1)

Simphson"s Rule:

0.25

Ex. No: 10   Write a C++ program to find the solution of y'=xz+2 and z'=-xy+5 using
Date: Runga-Kutta Simultaneous equation

AIM:

To find the solution for the above given equation using Runga-Kutta Simultaneous equation.

SOURCE CODE:

```
#include<iostream.h>

#include<conio.h>

#include<math.h>

#define f(x,y,z) (x*z+2)

#define g(x,y,z) (-x*y+5)

void main()

{

int i;

float h,k1,k2,k3,k4,l1,l2,l3,l4,x[10],y[10],z[10];

clrscr();

cout<<"Enter the initial values of x,y,z:"<<endl;

cin>>x[0]>>y[0]>>z[0];

cout<<"Enter the step size h:"<<endl;

cin>>h;

cout<<endl;

cout<<"Runga Kutta Method-Solution of equation"<<endl;

cout<<"y'=xz+2 and z'=xy+2"<<endl;

cout<<"x\t"<<"y\t\t"<<"z\t"<<endl;
```

```
for(i=0;i<10;i++)
{
k1=h*f(x[i],y[i],z[i]);
l1=h*g(x[i],y[i],z[i]);
k2=h*f((x[i]+h/2),(y[i]+k1/2),(z[i]+l1/2));
l2=h*g((x[i]+h/2),(y[i]+k1/2),(z[i]+l1/2));
k3=h*f((x[i]+h/2),(y[i]+k2/2),(z[i]+l2/2));
l3=h*g((x[i]+h/2),(y[i]+k2/2),(z[i]+l2/2));
k4=h*f((x[i]+h),(y[i]+k3),(z[i]+l3));
l4=h*g((x[i]+h),(y[i]+k3),(z[i]+l3));


y[i+1]=y[i]+(k1+2*k2+2*k3+k4)/6;
z[i+1]=z[i]+(l1+2*l2+2*l3+l4)/6;
x[i+1]=x[i]+h;


cout<<x[i+1]<<"\t"<<y[i+1]<<"\t"<<z[i+1]<<endl;
}
getch();
}
```

OUTPUT:

Enter the initial value x, y, z:

0   1   1

Enter the step size h:

0.05

Runga Kutta Method – Solution of Equations

y'=xz+2 and z'=-xy+5

x	y	z
0.05	1.101457	1.248666
0.1	1.206653	1.494318
0.15	1.316801	1.736412
0.2	1.433089	1.974362
0.25	1.556665	2.207526
0.3	1.688638	2.435197
0.35	1.830064	2.656592
0.4	1.981940	2.870840
0.45	2.145194	3.076976
0.5	2.220671	3.273932

Ex.no:11   Write a C++ program to find the solution of the equation y'=x*x+y/2 using

Date: Mline's Predicator and Correcter method

AIM:

To write a C++ program to find the solution for y'=x*x+y/2 using Mline's Predictor and Corrector

Method.

SOURCE CODE:

```cpp
#include<iostream.h>

#include<conio.h>

#include<math.h>

#define f(x,y) (pow(x,2)+y/2)

void main()

{

int i;

float h,c,x0,x1,2,x3,x4,y0,y1,y2,y3,yp,yc,f0,f1,f2,f3;

clrscr();

cout<<"Enter the first four values of x:"<<endl;

cin>>x0>>x1>>x2>>3;

cout<<"\n enter the corresponding four values of y:\n";

cin>>y0>>y1>>y2>>y3;

h=x1-x0;

cout<<"\n Mline predictor and corrector method\n";

cout<<"solution of y'=x*x+y/2\n";

for(i=1; i<8;i++)

{f1=f(x1,x2);

f2=f(x2,y2);
```

```
f3=f(x3,y3);

yp=y0+4*h*(2*f1-f2+2*f3)/3;

x4=x3+h;

c=y2+h*(f2+4*f3)/3;

line:

yc=c+h*f(x4,yp)/3;

if (fabs(yp-yc)<pow(10,-6)))

cout<<"\t"<<x4<<"\t"<<yc<<endl;

else

{yp=yc;

goto line;

}

x1=x2;

x2=x3;

x3=x4;

y0=y1;

y1=y2;

y2=y3;

y3=yc;

}

getch();

}
```

OUTPUT:

Enter the first four values of x:

1   1.1   1.2   1.3

Enter the corresponding four value of y:

2   2.2157   2.4398   2.7514

Milne's predictor corrector Method

solution of y'=x*x+y/2

X	Y
1.4	3.052827
1.5	3.450961
1.6	3.848582
1.7	4.35022
1.8	4.862447
1.9	5.487004
2	6.134192

Ex.no:12   **Write a program to find the solution of the equation y'=3e^x+2y using**

Date: **Euler's Method**

AIM:

To find the solution of the above given equation using Euler's Method.

SOURCE CODE:

```
#include<iostream.h>

#include<conio.h>

#include<math.h>

#include<iomanip.h>

#define f(x,y) (3*exp(x)+2*y)

vooid main()

{

int i;

float h,xn,x,ys,yi,ym,ye;

clrscr();

cout<<"Enter the intial value of x:"<<endl;

cin>>x;

cout<<"Enter the intial value of y:"<,endl;

cin>>ys;

cout<<"Enter the step size h:"<<endl;

cin>>h;

cout<<"_____
"<<endl;

cout<<"Euler's method  for solving y'=3*exp(x)+2*y"<<endl;

cout<<"x\t ysimple \t yimproved\t ymodified\t yextract"<<endl;
```

```
cout<<"_____
"<<endl;

yi=ym=ys;

for(i=1;i<11;i++)

{

ys=ys+h*f(x,ys);

xn=x+h;

yi=yi+(h/2)*(f(x,yi)+f(xn,yi+h*f(x,yi));

ym=ym+h*f(x+h/2,ym+(h/2)*f(x,ym));

ye=3*(exp(2*xn)-exp(xn));

cout<<setiosflags(ios::fixed)<<setprecision(6)<<xn<<"\t"<<ys<<"\t"<<setw(10)<<yi<<"\t"<<s
etw(10)

<<ym<<"\t"<<setw(10)<<ye<<endl;

x=xn;

}

getch();

}
```

OUTPUT:

Enter the intial value of x:

0

Enter the intial value of y:

0

Enter the step size h:

0.05

	Euler's Method of solving y'=3*exp(x)+2*y			
x	ysimple	yimproved	ymodified	yextract
0.05	0.15	0.157595	0.15754	0.161699
0.10	0.322691	0.339424	0.339321	0.34869
0.15	0.520735	0.548385	0.548218	0.564074
0.20	0.747084	0.787694	0.787454	0.811266
0.25	1.005003	1.06092	1.060597	1.41678
0.30	1.298107	1.372021	1.371602	1.41678

Ex.no:13   **Write a Program to find the solution of Laplace equation**

Date:

AIM:

To write a program to find solution of Laplace equation.

SOURCE CODE:

```cpp
#include<iostream.h>

#include<conio.h>

#include<math.h>

#include<generic.h>

void main()

{

int i,j,n;

float u[20][20],e,d[20][20],itn,un[20][20];

clrscr();

cout<<"Enter the no of sub squares in a row or column:"<<endl;

cin>>n;

cout<<"Enter the accuracy constant of e:"<<endl;

cin>>e;

cout<<"Enter the boundry value u(i,0) for all i:"<<endl;

for(i=0;i<n+1;i++)

cin>>u[i][0];

cout<<"Enter the boundry value u(i,"<<n<<") for all i"<<endl;

for(i=0;i<n+1;i++)

cin>>u[i][n];

cout<<"Enter the boundry values u(0,j) for all j"<<endl;

for(j=0;j<n+1;j++)
```

```cpp
cin>>u[0][j];
cout<<"Enter the boundry values u("<<n<<",i) for all j"<<endl;
for (j=0;j<n+1;j++)
cin>>u[n][j];
for(i=1;i<n;i++)
for(j=1;j<n;j++)
u[i][j]=0.0;
itn=0;
start:
itn++;
for(i=1;i<n;i++)
{
for(j=1;j<n;j++)
{
un[i][j]=(u[i-1][j]+u[i+1][j]+u[i][j-1]+u[i][j+1])/4;
d[i][j]=fabs(u[i][j]-un[i][j]);
}
}
for(i=1;i<n;i++)
for(j=1;j<n;j++)
if(d[i][j]>e)
goto line;
else
goto print;
line:
for(i=1;i<n;i++)
```

```cpp
for(j=1;j<n;j++)

u[i][j]=un[i][j];

goto start;

print:

cout<<endl;

cout<< "Solution of Laplace equation for interior lattice points"<<endl;

for(j=1;j<n;j++)

{

for(i=1;i<n;i++)

{

cout<<setiosflags(ios::fixed)<<setprecision(0)<<"u("<<i<<","<<j<<")="<<u[i][j]<<"\t";

}

cout<<endl;

}

cout<<"Convergence has occurred after "<<itn<<"iterations"<<endl;

getch();

}
```

OUTPUT:

Enter the no. of subsquares in a row or column:

4

Enter the accuracy constant of e:

0.0000001

Enter the boundary values of u(i,0) for all i

0   500   1000   500   0

Enter the boundary values of u(i,4) for all i

0   500   1000   500   0

Enter the boundary values of u(0,j) for all j

0   1000   2000   1000   0

Enter the boundary values of u(4,j) for all j

0   1000   2000   1000   0

Solution of Laplace equation for interior lattice points

u(1,1)=937.499878   u(2,1)=999.999817   u(3,1)=937.499878

u(1,2)=1249.999756   u(2,2)=1124.99756   u(3,2)=1249.99756

u(1,3)=937.499878   u(2,3)=999.999817   u(3,3)=937.499878

Convergence has occurred after 46 iterations.

Ex.no:14   **Write a Program to find the Temperature distribution of a given plate**

Date:

AIM:

To write a program to find the temperature distribution of a given plate.

SOURCE CODE:

```
#include<iostream.h>

#include<conio.h>

#include<math.h>

#include<generic.h>

void main()

{

int i,j,n;

float u[20][20],e,d[20][20],itn,un[20][20];

clrscr();

cout<<"Enter the no of sub units in a row or column:"<<endl;

cin>>n;

cout<<"Enter the accuracy constant :"<<endl;

cin>>e;

cout<<endl;

cout<<"enter the temperature u(i,0) for all i:"<<endl;

for(i=0;i<n+1;i++)

cin>>u[i][0];

cout<<"Enter the temperature  u(i,"<<n<<") for all i"<<endl;

for(i=0;i<n+1;i++)


cin>>u[i][n];
```

```cpp
cout<<"Enter the temperature u(0,j) for all j"<<endl;

for(j=0;j<n+1;j++)

cin>>u[0][j];

cout<<"Enter the temperature u("<<n<<",i) for all j"<<endl;

for (j=0;j<n+1;j++)

cin>>u[n][j];

for(i=1;i<n;i++)

{

for(j=1;j<n;j++)

{

u[i][j]=0.0;

itn=0;

}

}

start:

itn++;

for(i=1;i<n;i++)

{for(j=0;j<n;j++)

{un[i][j]=(u[i-1][j]+u[i+1][j]+u[i][j-1]+u[i][j+1])/4;

d[i][j]=fabs(u[i][j]-un[i][j]);

}

}

for(i=1;i<n;i++)

for(j=1;j<n;j++)

if(d[i][j]>e)

goto line;
```

```
else
goto print;
line:
for(i=1;i<n;i++)
for(j=1;j<n;j++)
u[i][j]=un[i][j];
goto start;
print:
cout<<endl;
cout<<"solution"<<endl;
for(i=1;i<n;i++)
{for(j=1;j<n;j++)
{
cout<<"u("<<i<<","<<j<<")="<<u[i][j]<<endl;
}
cout<<endl;
}
cout<<"values obtained after "<<itn<<"iteration"<<endl;
getch();
}
```

OUTPUT:

Enter the no of subunits in a row or column:

10

Enter the accuracy constant:0001

Enter the temperature   u(i,0) for all i:

100   100   100   100   100   100   100   100   100   100

Enter the temperature u(i,10) for all i:

20   20   20   20   20   20   20   20   20   20

Enter the temperature u(0,j) for all j:

0   0   0   0   0   0   0   0   0   0

Enter the temperature u(j,10)for all j:

0   0   0   0   0   0   0   0   0   0

this is the value obtained after 156 iteration

u(1,1)=49.167385   u(1,2)=68.000084   u(1,3)=76.150208   u(1,4)=79.730927

u(1,5)=80.760735   u(1,6)=79.730927   u(1,7)=49.167385   u(1,8)=68.000084

u(1,9)=49.167385

u(2,1)=28.66983   u(2,2)=46.683514   u(2,3)=56.878090   u(2,4)=62.013992

u(2,5)=63.582932   u(2,6)=62.013992   u(2,7)=56.878090   u(2,8)=46.683514

u(2,9)=28.66983

u(3,1)=18.829185   u(3,2)=33.194695   u(3,3)=42.637554   u(3,4)=47.874138

u(3,5)=49.543003   u(3,6)=47.874138   u(3,7)=42.637554   u(3,8)=33.194695

u(3,9)=18.829185

u(4,1)=13.453214   u(4,2)=24.630516   u(4,3)=32.613174   u(4,4)=37.305218

u(4,5)38.844654   u(4,6)=37.305218   u(4,7)=32.613774   u(4,8)=24.630516

u(4,9)=13.453214

u(5,1)=16.354382   u(5,2)=19.263205   u(5,3)=25.882629   u(5,4)=29.892517

u(5,5)=31.229145   u(5,6)=29.892517   u(5,7)=25.882629   u(5,8)=19.263205

u(5,9)=16.354382

u(6,1)=8.702339   u(6,2)=16.187754   u(6,3)=21.764841   u(6,4)=25.157055

u(6,5)=26.290882   u(6,6)=25.157055   u(6,7)=21.764841   u(6,8)=16.187754

u(6,9)=8.702339

u(7,1)=8.268451   u(7,2)=15.022826   u(7,3)=19.835146   u(7,4)=22.683584 u(7,5)=23.624252   u(7,6)=22.683584   u(7,7)=19.835146   u(7,8)=15.022826

u(7,9)=8.268451

u(8,1)=9.3496   u(8,2)=15.802076   u(8,3)=19.87191   u(8,4)=22.121105

u(8,5)=22.842182   u(8,6)=22.121105   u(8,7)=19.87191   u(8,8)=15.802076

u(8,9)=9.3496

u(9,1)=13.328632   u(9,2)=18.965313   u(9,3)=21.7313   u(9,4)=23.088976

u(9,5)=23.504725   u(9,6)=23.088976   u(9,7)=21.7313   u(9,8)=18.965313

u(9,9)=13.328632